IAN 2 8 1999 DATE DUE

BL N/A
BOND
N/A

D1542317

FUTURE FILES

CITIES IN THE SKY

A BEGINNER'S GUIDE TO LIVING IN SPACE

SARAH
ANGLISS
and
COLIN
UTTLEY

COPPER BEECH BOOKS
BROOKFIELD, CONNECTICUT

© Aladdin Books Ltd 1998

Designed and produced by
Aladdin Books Ltd
28 Percy Street
London W1P 0LD

First published in the United States in 1998 by
Copper Beech Books,
an imprint of
The Millbrook Press
2 Old New Milford Road
Brookfield, Connecticut 06804

Editor
Simon Beecroft

Design
David West
Children's Book Design

Designer
Malcolm Smythe

Picture Research
Brooks Krikler Research

Illustrators
Stephen Sweet, Stuart Squires (Simon Girling
Associates), Ross Watton, Alex Pang, Pat Murray

Printed in Belgium
All rights reserved

Library of Congress Cataloging-in-Publication Data
Uttley, Colin.
Cities in the sky : a beginner's guide to living in space / by
Colin Uttley and Sarah Angliss ; illustrated by Stephen Sweet,
Stuart Squires, Ross Watton, Alex Pang, Pat Murray.
p. cm. — (Future files)
Includes index.
Summary: Speculates on the lifestyles, food, interpersonal
relations, health aspects, and technology of life in space
stations and in colonies on other planets.
ISBN 0-7613-0822-9 (lib. bdg.). —
ISBN 0-7613-0741-9 (pb)
1. Space colonies—Juvenile literature. 2. Space station—
Juvenile literature. 3. Space environment—Juvenile literature.
[1. Space colonies. 2. Space stations.] I. Angliss, Sarah. II.
Rockwood, Richard, ill.
III. Pang, Alex, ill. IV. Title. V. Series.
TL795.7U88 1998   98-21352
629.44'2—dc21   CIP AC
5 4 3 2 1

J 629.442 Ang
00890 1764 01/12/99   BON
Angliss, Sarah

Cities in the sky : by
Angliss, Sarah and

AP

AP

LEROY COLLINS
LEON COUNTY PUBLIC LIBRARY
TALLAHASSEE, FLORIDA 32301

...ON CONTROL

INTRODUCTION

As the earth becomes more overcrowded and increasingly more polluted, we may need to find new places to call home. We've already started planning new settlements away from this planet. Future generations may spend their entire lives in these cities in the sky.

The first humans to live away from Earth inhabited cramped space stations (*see* page 6-7). Early in the 21st century, a community of astronauts will be living in the International Space Station (ISS), an orbiting complex of laboratories and dwellings.

But the ISS will be dwarfed by tomorrow's space stations — city-sized vessels that may spin to create artificial gravity (*see* pages 8-9).

Perhaps the inhabitants of these giant space-homes will leave Earth's orbit altogether — finding their own destiny as they colonize another planet.

While astronomers scan the skies for distant planets that may support life as Earth does, colonization of new worlds may begin closer to home, with the moon (*see* pages 12-13) or Mars (*see* pages 14-15).

How will settlers survive in these empty environments? Will they live in airtight bases breathing an artificial atmosphere? Or will they find ways to change the environment of a whole planet so it resembles Earth's? What will people do on other planets (*see* pages 16-17)?

In the 20th century, we saw the first people in space — the big challenge for the next century is to find ways to inhabit new worlds.

Right *Need to tell science fact from science fiction? Take a look at our Reality Check boxes. We can't see into the future, but these devices tell you how realistic an idea is. The more green lights, the better. The "how soon?" line guesses when in the future the idea might become reality: Each green light is 50 years (so in the example here, it's 100 years in the future).*

REALITY CHECK

FEASIBLE TECHNOLOGY	○	○	○	○	○
SCIENCE IS SOUND	○	○	○	○	○
AFFORDABLE	○	○	○	○	○
HOW SOON?	○	○	○	○	○

MOBILE HOMES

Unlike spacecraft that journey to particular places, like the moon or Mars, space stations remain in empty space. They provide homes for astronauts who are carrying out experiments. In the future, space stations could also become the departure terminals for missions to other planets. As the cost of getting into space comes down, people may start taking vacations aboard one!

Left *A city that hovers above the surface of Earth, as New York does in this 1929 sci-fi magazine, would be expensive to build and run. A more practical idea would be to build a city that orbited Earth, using space station technology.*

THE NEXT GENERATION

Launched in 1986, the *Mir* space station is now an aging piece of space technology. It will be replaced by the International Space Station (ISS, *far right*). Built jointly by space agencies in the United States, Russia, Canada, Japan, and Europe, it will welcome its first crew in 1999, and is due for completion in 2002.

SPACE LAB

The astronauts inside the ISS will learn more about the effects of living in space, and will research new medicines and test new materials. They will also try out new ways of recycling space station waste (*see* pages 20-21).

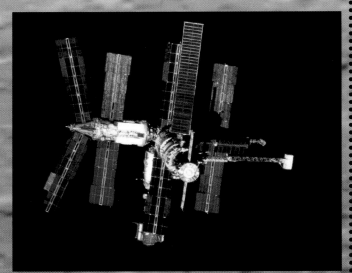

Above *Seven years after its mission was due to end, the* Mir *space station is still in orbit. ISS crews visit it for training.*

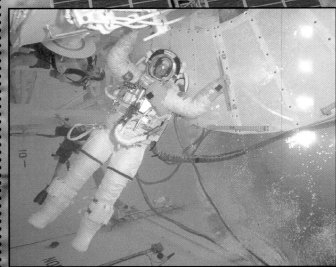

Above *During training, ISS crew members submerge themselves in huge water tanks. These give a feeling similar to floating in space.*

BIG IDEA

In orbit 217 miles above Earth, the ISS will be the largest object ever assembled in space. Astronauts will float through an area the size of two jumbo jets as they go about their work. Because of its size, the station will be assembled in space from five different parts — a central core, a propulsion and control section, living quarters, and two laboratories.

THE ISS

FEASIBLE TECHNOLOGY	○	○	○	○	○
SCIENCE IS SOUND	○	○	○	○	○
AFFORDABLE	○	○	○	○	○
HOW SOON?	○	○	○	○	○

TOUCHING BASE

Above *An astronaut on board* Skylab, *the first US space station, takes a shower in zero gravity.*

As they orbit the Earth or drift through empty space, astronauts don't feel a force of gravity pulling them downwards. We say they are experiencing 'zero gravity'. This is why they float around, which can be awkward when they are trying to work, eat or even sleep. Without gravity, it can be difficult to know which way up you are. Scientists want to find ways to create a force just like Earth's gravity artificially, making a space station feel more like home.

GRAVITONS
Just as light is made of particles (tiny pieces of matter) called photons, scientists think there could be particles that create gravity. Even though scientists have given these particles a name – gravitons – they are still trying to actually discover one.

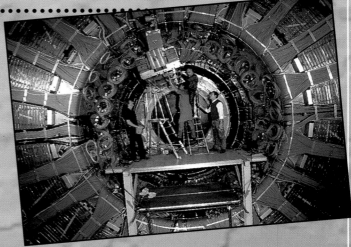

Above *Scientists hope to discover gravitons (individual particles of gravity) using machines called particle accelerators. These machines smash together particles of matter at almost the speed of light, creating new particles and bursts of energy.*

GRAVITY BEAM
If scientists can find gravitons, they may be able to create gravity on board space stations. Then space stations would be more comfortable places to live. They could even become orbiting hotels, where guests could turn the force of gravity up or down as easily as the air-conditioning, in places like a gym.

Right *For a few seconds, passengers feel weightless as this aircraft climbs into the air and then dives towards Earth. It is used by astronauts in training to give them a feel for zero gravity. Weightlessness in space can be damaging to astronauts' bodies: without the force of gravity on them, their bones and muscles can waste away.*

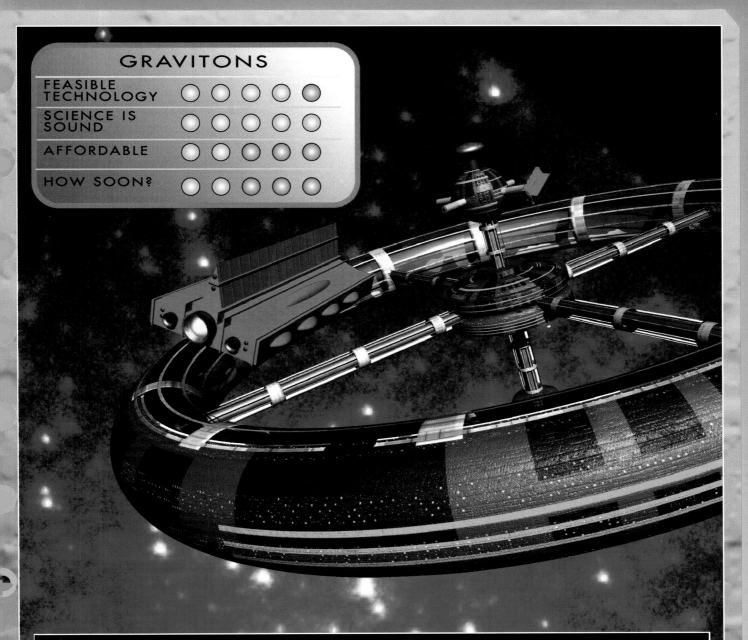

GRAVITONS

FEASIBLE TECHNOLOGY	○	○	○	○	●
SCIENCE IS SOUND	○	○	○	○	○
AFFORDABLE	○	○	○	○	
HOW SOON?	○	○	○	○	

IN A SPIN

The scientist and science-fiction writer Arthur C. Clarke imagined a future space station as a majestic spinning wheel (above). This was one way to generate artificial gravity. A spinning craft would create a force that would push objects towards its outside wall, just like the clothes in a tumble drier. People inside the craft would be pushed towards this wall, so they could walk along it as if it were the floor (right). If the craft rotated at the right speed, this force would be the same as the force of gravity on Earth.

GETTING UP THERE

Early spacecraft were thrown away after just one journey, so going into space was hugely expensive. If we are going to begin to live in space, we need to find a cheaper way of getting there and back.

WHAT A WASTE

When the United States sent astronauts to the Moon in the 1960s and 1970s, nearly all the hardware it used was dumped in space or allowed to burn up in the atmosphere. The Space Shuttle, launched in 1981, was the first reusable spacecraft. But even the Shuttle throws away its massive fuel tank after every trip, and it hasn't brought down the cost of space travel at all.

Over the next century, a new generation of reusable space vehicles will cut the cost of going into space by about 90 per cent. Called Reusable Launch Vehicles (RLVs), they're still in the early stages of development – but the first prototypes will be flying soon.

Above *Flying saucers were the RLVs of science fiction. Unlike ordinary spacecraft, they could repeatedly take off and land.*

STAR TURN

The first RLV, *Venture Star*, is now being tested. Like the Space Shuttle, it takes off vertically and glides back to Earth to land like an aeroplane. *Venture Star* uses a new type of engine called an aerospike. It uses this rocket for every stage of its journey, unlike conventional spacecraft.

Below *RLVs will soon make journeys into space routine. Used to launch satellites and supply space stations, they will often travel without a human crew.*

Above *Using a space station as a base, RLVs could be used in the exploration of Mars. They could shuttle people and goods to and from the surface of the planet.*

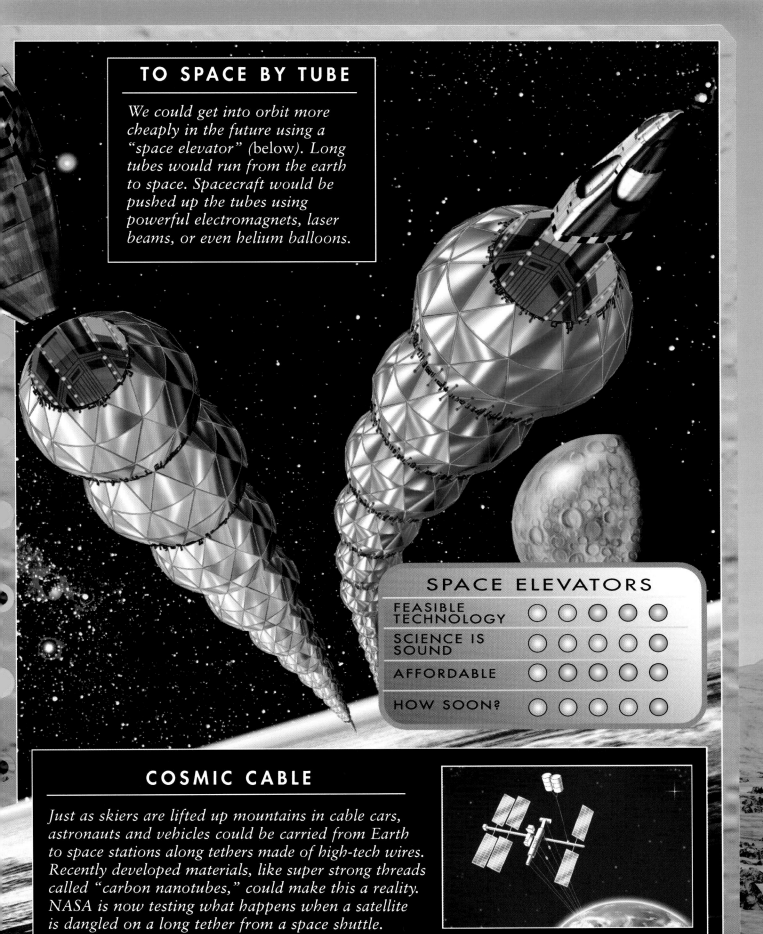

TO SPACE BY TUBE

We could get into orbit more cheaply in the future using a "space elevator" (below). Long tubes would run from the earth to space. Spacecraft would be pushed up the tubes using powerful electromagnets, laser beams, or even helium balloons.

SPACE ELEVATORS

FEASIBLE TECHNOLOGY	○	○	○	○	○
SCIENCE IS SOUND	○	○	○	○	○
AFFORDABLE	○	○	○	○	○
HOW SOON?	○	○	○	○	○

COSMIC CABLE

Just as skiers are lifted up mountains in cable cars, astronauts and vehicles could be carried from Earth to space stations along tethers made of high-tech wires. Recently developed materials, like super strong threads called "carbon nanotubes," could make this a reality. NASA is now testing what happens when a satellite is dangled on a long tether from a space shuttle.

TO THE MOON

When astronaut Eugene Cernan climbed back into the *Apollo 17* spacecraft in 1972, he was sure that others would return to build a moon base within a decade. But nearly thirty years later, he is still the last person to walk on the moon. Recently, ice has been discovered at the moon's poles — just what we need to sustain life on a lunar station. This has made scientists dream again about building a base on the moon.

TAPPING IN

If there really is water in the moon's polar craters, then we have an ingredient for an ideal home. Lunar dwellers could drink it, grow food with it, and use it to make oxygen and hydrogen. These gases would be excellent rocket fuels for journeys back to Earth. Oxygen could also be used to make a breathable atmosphere on the base.

Above *The discovery of what could be a fossil from Mars made many scientists want to set up base there. But scientists who found lunar ice think we should be designing a colony for the moon first.*

A ROOM WITH A VIEW

A lunar colony could be big for business. In the moon's low gravity, companies could build high-tech materials with unusual properties and develop new ways to make medicines. A Japanese organization wants to run a Lunar Olympics. Funded by people gambling on each event, these games would be held in a giant, air-filled dome. Meanwhile, the Hilton Hotel Corporation has made plans for a lunar hotel.

Above top *At the turn of the century, visiting the moon was just a fantasy. Less than 70 years later, the Apollo missions made the dream a reality (above bottom).*

Above *The Lunar Rover enabled Apollo astronauts to venture away from their spacecraft. A future moon base would see the development of a new generation of vehicles.*

MOON BASE

FEASIBLE TECHNOLOGY	○	○	○	○	●
SCIENCE IS SOUND	○	○	○	○	○
AFFORDABLE	○	○	○	○	○
HOW SOON?	○	○	○	○	○

LUNAR HOTEL

A proposed hotel on the moon, the Lunar Hilton would be 1,006 feet high, with 5,000 rooms and its own beach and sea. Huge solar panels would supply the hotel with energy.

LIFE ON MARS • Will humans live on Mars?

Mars is a strong candidate for providing humans with a new home. First visited by unmanned probes in the 1960s, Mars has been the object of renewed interest since the 1997 *Mars Pathfinder* mission. Over the next decade, many more missions are planned — to be followed, eventually, by the first human visitors.

TERRAFORMING MARS

Future humans could live on Mars if a technique called "terraforming" is used to alter its climate (*far right*). Mirrors would be placed in orbit around Mars to reflect the sun's rays, melting the planet's ice caps to release carbon dioxide and water vapor. These would form lakes, warm the atmosphere, and make a home for microorganisms.

Right *Visitors to the first Martian bases will need to wear clumsy space suits. But if terraforming is successful, they will eventually be able to explore the surface in ordinary clothes.*

Above *Biosphere II, in Arizona, is a miniworld inside a huge, sealed greenhouse. It helps us to find out how to sustain life on other planets.*

A CLOSER LOOK

The 1997, *Pathfinder* mission used a remote-control wheeled vehicle, *Sojourner* (*below*), to investigate the planet. It found rounded pebbles and other evidence that Mars was once warm and wet. The next Mars mission, *Surveyor '98*, will measure the amount of water and carbon dioxide in the ice caps. It will also provide more information about the planet's climate.

OVER AND OUT

Mars Observer (below) *was launched in 1992 to map the Martian surface for future exploration. All went well on its journey to Mars – but when its engines were fired to put it into orbit around the planet, it went dead. The probe was probably ruined by an on-board explosion.*

TERRAFORMED MARS

FEASIBLE TECHNOLOGY	○ ○ ○ ○ ○
SCIENCE IS SOUND	○ ○ ○ ○ ○
AFFORDABLE	○ ○ ○ ○ ○
HOW SOON?	○ ○ ○ ○ ○

CITY LIFE ·

Great cities like New York and Rome weren't built in a day — and a city on another planet may also take centuries to flourish. The first generation of interplanetary settlers may feel uneasy adapting to life on an alien planet. But over time, communities, homes, and industries will develop. Future generations born there will consider it home.

PLANETARY RESEARCH

What will people actually do on a new world? Apart from growing food (*see* pages 18-19), the most important jobs will probably be research into conditions on the new planet. Experimenting on the atmosphere of another planet should reveal a lot about how the atmosphere on Earth works, too. Governments and companies will pay people to do this research for them.

Above *As this magazine cover shows, colonists on new worlds may need to export animals from Earth.*

NEW INDUSTRY

Mining could also be a huge industry — one that is more profitable than any other industry humans have created. A new planet could be a rich source of minerals that are rare on Earth. Colonists could mine these materials and sell them.

Space rocks, called asteroids, may also be good sources of rare metals and other useful substances. Large asteroids could be towed into orbit around Earth or Mars. People could land on them, then build mines to extract valuable materials.

SPORTING LIFE

If our new home has low gravity, our athletic prowess would seem better than ever. We could jump, dive, kick balls, or tumble farther than any record breaker on Earth.

Above *Permanent bases on Mars will only be developed once it has been proved that people can survive for long periods on the planet. The first cities will develop from scientific bases.*

Above *Although the scientific facilities on board the space shuttle are cramped, they have allowed space scientists to develop technologies that will be used on the moon or Mars.*

MARS SCIENTISTS

The first settlers on another planet, such as Mars, will be full-time space scientists. They will need to find out as much as possible about the planet they are planning to live on, taking about 16 months to complete the 75-million-mile trip around the planet. This information will be used to plan the location of cities.

WORKING COLONY

FEASIBLE TECHNOLOGY	○	○	○	○	○
SCIENCE IS SOUND	○	○	○	○	○
AFFORDABLE	○	○	○	○	○
HOW SOON?	○	○	○	○	○

SPACE FUEL · Feeding a future space colony

To sustain a colony on another planet, we will need to grow crops. We could do this in the open air as soon as a planet has been terraformed (*see* page 14). Before then, we would have to grow food in a sealed living station called a "biosphere."

UNDER ONE ROOF
A biosphere is a transparent dome that can support a colony of plants, insects, and humans. One has already been built in Arizona, (*see* page 14). Called Biosphere II (the earth itself is "Biosphere I"), it was used to test how different environments react inside a sealed system. Once a biosphere is sealed, it should not need to be replenished with fresh nutrients or air. The life sustained within it creates a balanced ecosystem, recycling and exchanging nutrients and gases, just as the plants and animals do on Earth.

CRASH TEST
Arizona's biosphere was able to sustain eight people — but it had to be reopened after a year because its air ran short of oxygen.

Below In the 1971 movie Silent Running, *the earth has been devastated by nuclear war, killing all crops. Food is grown in spacecraft in Saturn's orbit.*

Above *Scientists can alter plants' genes (chemicals that help determine how they develop) to make them more pest-resistant. Genetic engineering could help crops survive on new planets.*

NO SECOND CHANCE
In space, there may be no way to rescue a failing biosphere — each one would have to be a failsafe home for a human colony.

Below *This* Skylab *astronaut is mixing dried food into a paste. Early space food like this was tasteless and dull.*

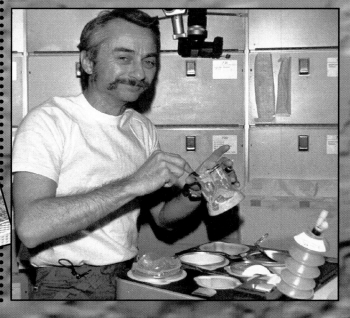

HYDROPONICS

Space stations and colonies will not have soil, but crops could be nurtured in tanks of gravel and water. The roots of each plant are suspended in the gravel, which has been enriched with minerals the plant needs. This tried-and-tested growing method is called "hydroponics."

Nutrients

GROWING FOOD

FEASIBLE TECHNOLOGY	○	○	○	○	○
SCIENCE IS SOUND	○	○	○	○	○
AFFORDABLE	○	○	○	○	○
HOW SOON?	○	○	○	○	○

SPACE JUNK •

Left *Not all space garbage is left in orbit. Out-of-date or faulty satellites can be picked up by the Space Shuttle and carried back down to Earth. They can then be dismantled for spare parts, recycled, or even sold to collectors. These old Soviet Sputnik satellites were auctioned in 1996.*

Space flight produces a lot of waste. The number of dead satellites, used rocket boosters, and other pieces of junk in orbit around Earth has doubled over the past 5 years to roughly 8,000 in total. This garbage could block our path into space, damage satellite equipment, or affect the forthcoming International Space Station (*see* page 6).

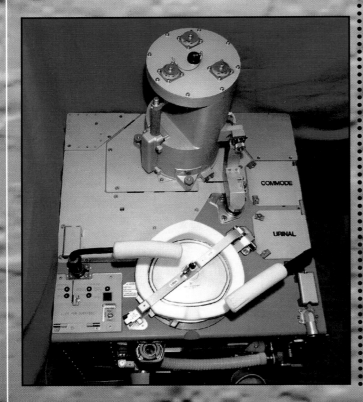

CLEAN SWEEP
Pieces of junk falling back to Earth could trigger missile early-warning systems. Scientists are now beginning to find ways to avoid this extremely dangerous scenario. The Japanese, for example, are building a radar that can search the skies for garbage. This $9.2 million scanner will also keep an eye out for asteroids approaching Earth. Russia is building a space-junk scanner of their own, called *Globus II*. Cased inside a 200-foot-high dome, it may also be used to trace enemy aircraft.

LIFE AFTER DEATH
Many dead satellites contain valuable microchips. At the moment it would be very expensive to capture and recycle them. However, in centuries to come, we may be discarding worn-out space stations the size of cities. As more people have access to space, these dumped hulks could be taken over by squatters. They might even become places where interplanetary criminals could hide.

Left *On spacecraft and space stations, toilets are known as waste collection systems (WCS). Astronauts sit on them as normal, but air suction is used to counteract the effects of weightlessness. This one is used aboard the space shuttle* Endeavour.

NEARLY NEW

If a future space station was situated far from Earth, new equipment could be hard to come by, so it would make sense to recycle things. "Scavengers" could travel between space stations, bartering materials, and secondhand machines.

JUNK SCAVENGERS

FEASIBLE TECHNOLOGY	○	○	○	○	○
SCIENCE IS SOUND	○	○	○	○	○
AFFORDABLE	○	○	○	○	○
HOW SOON?	○	○	○	○	○

MEET THE NEIGHBORS

The universe may well be teeming with life. So as we set up home on a remote planet, we may come into contact with some extraterrestrial hosts. Scientists called xenobiologists have speculated what aliens might be like. There is no reason to believe they will be at all like us. For example, the basic material that forms all currently known living things is the chemical element carbon. Aliens, however, could be based on another material, such as silicon, or they may even exist as pure energy.

DON'T GO CHANGING

Before we terraform a planet to sustain a human colony (*see* page 14), we must make sure no other creature thrives there. Otherwise, we might change that alien lifeform's home environment so it no longer supports them — making us very unwelcome guests.

LIFE LINE

Just like us, aliens will be perfectly adapted to live on their home planet. For example, if they evolved on a planet that has a much stronger gravity than Earth, they would feel far greater forces pulling them down. They may have developed a supporting structure that is far stronger than our skeleton. This could be in the form of a tough outer shell (*far right*).

Above *In the movie* Men in Black *(1997), aliens are already with us — but special agents ("Men in Black") keep the public from knowing.*

SPEAK YOUR LANGUAGE

If our neighbors are intelligent, we may be able to talk with them — but only if we can translate between our different languages. That's assuming aliens use any form of language at all. Speech experts today are barely able to make machines that can translate between languages on Earth. Translating one that developed independently from human speech will be even harder.

Left *In the science-fiction movie* Mars Attacks!, *aliens from a neighboring planet are far from friendly. These creatures use a "talking machine" to translate their language and assure the earth they have come in peace. But their actions tell a different story as they speed around the planet on a trail of destruction.*

ALIEN DETECTOR

FEASIBLE TECHNOLOGY	○	○	○	○	○
SCIENCE IS SOUND	○	○	○	○	○
AFFORDABLE	○	○	○	○	○
HOW SOON?	○	○	○	○	○

LOOK! NO HANDS

Cute aliens in the movie Explorers *(1985, right) have bodies that look and work much like our own. But creatures that evolve on a planet dissimilar to Earth are unlikely to have our size and shape (above). Scientists are still not certain whether there are any other Earthlike planets, but they are looking for them around distant stars. Closer to home, aliens could well be microbes — simple, rugged microscopic life-forms able to develop on inhospitable planets and moons.*

CRADLE TO GRAVE

Rituals and beliefs help people make sense of the cycle of life, including sickness and health. Space explorers of the future may want to worship their gods, get married, and dispose of their dead just as we do at home. But there may be some changes, too — for example, in the way that medicine is practiced.

NEW GODS

Before he became the second person ever to step on the moon, astronaut Buzz Aldrin took out some wine and bread. As a Catholic, he would not set foot on an alien world without first taking Holy Communion.

Human settlers on new planets will bring their beliefs from Earth, but new ones may also develop, such as worshiping a new star.

SAFE PRACTICE

Medicine will have to cope with the threat of new forms of illness. When the first astronauts returned to Earth after stepping on the moon, they were separated from their families and friends and locked in a sealed room. This quarantine was a safety measure in case they had picked up any "moon bugs."

Above *The 1956 movie* Forbidden Planet *shows just two people (a father and his daughter) and a robot living together on a deserted planet.*

MUTANT BUGS

These astronauts came back healthy, but future space colonists might not be so lucky. Even if their new home was free from microbes when they arrived, they may unwittingly carry some from Earth. And if an environment has high levels of radiation, these microbes could begin to mutate, producing new diseases.

Left *This hologram doctor in the television series* Star Trek Voyager *is a sci-fi idea of futuristic medicine. In reality, a computer could be programmed just to make a diagnosis and give advice after asking a list of questions.*

Right *As the creator of* Star Trek, *Gene Roddenberry spent a lifetime at the forefront of science fiction. It is fitting that he was laid to rest in space. At his own request, his ashes were loaded into the nose cone of a small rocket and blasted off on a journey to the "final frontier."*

TELEMEDICINE

Settlers on a space station or another planet may not always have a surgeon on hand. People who need an operation will have to visit a telemedicine suite (below). This links them to a surgeon in another suite that could be thousands of miles away. Using virtual-reality technology (in which realistic, 3D scenes are produced by computer, right), the surgeon can "feel" and "see" the patient, as if they were in the same room. Robot arms and hands around the patient follow every move the surgeon makes. A few specialized operations have already been performed this way.

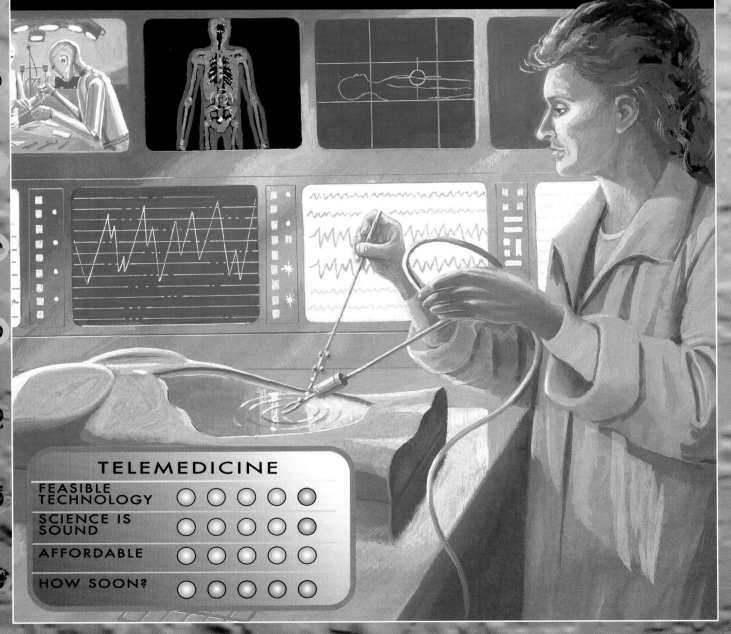

TELEMEDICINE

FEASIBLE TECHNOLOGY	○	○	○	○	
SCIENCE IS SOUND	○	○	○	○	
AFFORDABLE	○	○	○	○	
HOW SOON?	○	○	○	○	

PHONE HOME.
Calling long-distance

Space stations and colonies could be lonely places. The people who live on them will want to keep in touch with Earth. There's no problem relaying messages to and from stations in Earth's orbit. But for people living farther apart, there will be problems with instant communication such as telephone calls.

LIGHT-SPEED
Electromagnetic waves, such as beams of light or radio, are the fastest things in the universe. We use them to send messages as swiftly as possible. But even these waves travel too slowly to let you chat with someone a few billion miles away.

FAST TALK
It would take at least four minutes for the voice of someone living on Mars to travel to Earth — even though it would be sent by radio. It would take another four minutes to hear a reply, so conversation between Mars and Earth would be very slow. Chatting between a moon of Jupiter and Earth would be even slower. This planet is 310 million miles away, so every word would take 40 minutes to travel one way.

Above *In the 1968 movie* 2001 — A Space Odyssey, *astronauts use this machine to watch video messages recorded by their family back on Earth.*

SLOW GOING
Instead of being able to have a conversation on a telephone, people on distant planets will have to record a message, send it by fax or e-mail, and wait for an answer. So, in the future, we'll be using the equivalent of the postal service!

KEEPING IN TOUCH

Humans need the touch of their loved ones, as well as their pictures and the sound of their voices. This device, called a "dataglove," already allows people on the Internet to feel as if they are holding hands. Scientists are hoping one day to develop touch simulators that plug directly into the brain. In the future, we may use them to "touch" each other across space. We could still only touch like this over relatively short distances since time delay would cause problems (see above).

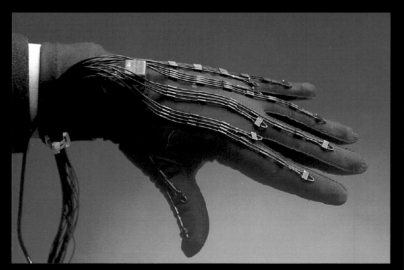

INTERPLANETARY PHONE

FEASIBLE TECHNOLOGY	◯	◯	◯	◯	◯
SCIENCE IS SOUND	◯	◯	◯	◯	◯
AFFORDABLE	◯	◯	◯	◯	◯
HOW SOON?	◯	◯	◯	◯	◯

LIGHT-SPEED

Some scientists are trying to break the ultimate speed barrier — the speed of light. Only minute particles can travel faster than light — except in sci-fi movies, where spaceships, like this one in Event Horizon *(1997), cross vast distances at "light-speed."*

BAILING OUT. Lifeboats in space

If there is an emergency on a space station, the crew may need to bail out. They must have an escape plan ready, since there won't be time to send help from Earth. Astronauts on the *Mir* space station have a small *Soyuz* spaceship ready in case of trouble. But new, specialized systems are set to replace this.

Above *Providing vital oxygen and protection from fire, space suits are always worn by astronauts during launch and reentry.*

DOWN TO EARTH

Future space stations will be so big, the crew might not have time to reach an escape craft in an emergency. But they may be able to leap to safety in extra-protective space suits topped by thin metal parachutes. Using boosters to reenter Earth's atmosphere, these space suits will protect them from the scorching 3,600°F temperature.

Above *In 1970, an on-board explosion forced the Apollo 13 crew to turn back. They used the engines of their lunar lander to return to Earth.*

LIFEBOAT

The International Space Station (*see* page 6) will have its own emergency craft, called crew return vehicles (CRVs). These will be in the form of "lifting bodies" — craft that have no wings but use their bodies to provide lift. CRVs will be inexpensive and easy to get into space. They will carry up to six passengers, and will be steered back to Earth just like ordinary aircraft.

Right *In 1997, a fire on board Mir, followed by a collision and a computer failure, nearly resulted in the crew abandoning the space station.*

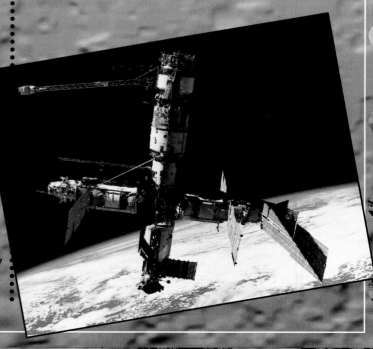

DEEP-SPACE RESCUE

FEASIBLE TECHNOLOGY	○	○ ○	○	○
SCIENCE IS SOUND	○	○ ○	○	○
AFFORDABLE	○	○ ○	○	○
HOW SOON?	○	○ ○	○	○

NO ONE CAN HEAR YOU SCREAM

Billions of miles from home, with a deadly predator on board, the heroine of the movie Alien *(1979) escapes to a mini-shuttle that's attached to her ship. Craft in deep space will need "lifeboats" like these, in which people can survive until help arrives — from the nearest inhabited planet or space station.*

GLOSSARY

APOLLO
The series of U.S. space missions that took the first people to the moon in the late 1960s and early 1970s.

ATMOSPHERE
A blanket of gases that surrounds a planet.

BIOSPHERE
A sealed transparent dome, containing breathable gases, that is completely cut off from the outside world. Plants and animals can thrive in a biosphere, as they can on Earth.

DEEP SPACE
The regions of space that lie beyond our own solar system (the group of planets, moons, and other bodies, including the earth, that orbit the sun).

ECOSYSTEM
A group of plants and animals that thrive together, exchanging nutrients and gases with each other. Life on Earth forms a natural ecosystem.

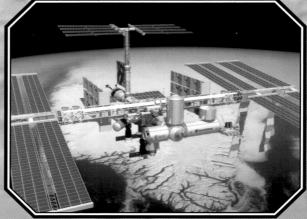

ELECTROMAGNETIC WAVES
Waves of energy that travel at 188,000 miles per second — faster than anything else in the universe — and can move through empty space. Light, radio waves, and X rays are all types of electromagnetic wave.

GENETIC ENGINEERING
Using technology to alter the "genes" of a living thing. Genes are the chemical instructions at the heart of every one of its cells that determine how it lives and develops.

GRAVITONS
Particles that are supposed to create gravity, just as photons create light. Scientists are still searching for gravitons.

GRAVITY
The force that exists between any two masses, pulling them together. Gravity between yourself and Earth pulls you toward the ground.

HOLOGRAM
An apparently three-dimensional image produced on a photographic plate or film.

INTERNATIONAL SPACE STATION (ISS)
Due for completion in 2002, this will be the largest-ever space station, built by the space agencies of the United States, Russia, Japan, Canada, Europe, and other nations.

INTERNET
A vast network of computers that we can use to send words, pictures, sounds, and moving images to each other around the world.

JUPITER
The largest planet in our solar system (the planets, moons, and other bodies that orbit the sun). Jupiter is the fifth planet from the sun and is made mainly of gas.

LUNAR ROVER
A battery-powered lightweight two-seater buggy that Apollo astronauts drove across the moon in 1972.

MARS
The closest planet to Earth, and a likely destination for a future space colony. Mars is the fourth planet from the sun.

MICROBES
Very simple life forms. Some microbes can survive in hostile environments — they have even been known to survive on the moon for two and a half years.

MICROCHIP
A sliver of silicon, about the size of a postage stamp, that can have millions of simple electronic circuits etched onto its surface. There are microchips at the heart of every modern computer.

MIR
The space station launched by the former U.S.S.R. in 1986 and now being used by International Space Station (ISS) astronauts for training.

NANOTUBE
An extremely strong, fine thread made of a special type of carbon called a fullerine. Nanotubes could be used to tether space stations to Earth.

PARTICLE ACCELERATOR
A tube that accelerates (speeds up) particles inside it to almost the speed of light. Scientists smash particles together in this machine to investigate the tiny particles of the universe.

PHOTONS
Tiny particles that make up light.

QUARANTINE
A place where people or other living things are isolated from the outside world to prevent them from spreading diseases.

RADAR
A system that bounces radio waves off objects to find out where they are. Radar is used to detect pieces of space junk that orbit the earth.

SKYLAB
An early American space station, built in the 1970s, which used an old rocket case as the living area.

SOYUZ
A Russian spacecraft that ferries cosmonauts (Russian astronauts) to and from the *Mir* space station. It will also be used to ferry people to and from the International Space Station.

SPACE ELEVATOR
A tether that could connect a space station to Earth, enabling people and equipment to move up and down it just like an elevator.

SPACE JUNK
Scrapped satellites and burnt-out rocket boosters that orbit the earth. This junk may damage spacecraft, including the International Space Station.

SPACE SHUTTLE
A reusable space plane that is used to launch satellites, send experiments into space, and ferry astronauts to and from space stations.

SPEED OF LIGHT
Light travels at 188,000 miles per second through empty space. Radio messages also travel through space at this speed.

TELEMEDICINE
A system that uses communication links to let a doctor or surgeon treat patients remotely, even millions of miles away.

TERRAFORMING
Changing the conditions on a planet, such as the gases in its atmosphere, to make it more like Earth.

ZERO GRAVITY
A term used to describe a place, such as in empty space or in orbit around a planet, where people feel no force of gravity. This makes them feel weightless.

INDEX

PHOTO CREDITS
Abbreviations: t-*top*, m-*middle*,
b-*bottom*, r-*right*, l-*left*, c-*center*
Cover ml, 8tr & b, 9b, 14m, 15br,
16br, 18t, 26b & back cover –
Frank Spooner Pictures. Cover br, 4,
6b both, 8tl, 9t, 10b both, 12t & b,
16bl, 17, 18br, 20b, 28 all, 30 & 32
– NASA. 6t, 12m & 16t – Mary
Evans Picture Library. 10t, 18bl,
24br & 29 – Kobal Collection. 14t –
Science Photo Library. 20t – Rex
Features. 22t – Columbia/ Tristar
(courtesy Kobal). 22b – Warner Bros
(courtesy Kobal). 23 & 24bl – Para-
mount Pictures (courtesy Kobal). 24t
& 26t – MGM (courtesy Kobal). 25
– Glaxo Wellcome. 27 – Cinesite
(courtesy Kobal).